Mick Manning & Brita Granström

Drama SCHOOL

F

FRANCES LINCOLN
CHILDREN'S BOOKS

For Ms Sheen, my excellent English teacher – M.M.
For my cousins – B.G.

Text and illustrations copyright © Mick Manning and Brita Granström 1999
First published in 1999 by Kingfisher, an imprint of Larousse plc

This edition published in Great Britain and in the USA in 2009 by
Frances Lincoln Children's Books, 4 Torriano Mews,
Torriano Avenue, London NW5 2RZ
www.franceslincoln.com

British Library Cataloguing in Publication Data
available on request

ISBN 978-1-84507-845-4

Printed in China

9 8 7 6 5 4 3 2 1

Contents

What this book is about

Drama is the art of producing an entertaining show. In this book you'll learn how to build a puppet theatre, make a movie and put on a play, plus loads of other things to dazzle your friends and family.

Hello I'm Brita! Get ready to enrol in your first drama class...

funny hats

old clothes

Paper

old tights

bag

shoes

4

Useful things

You'll need lots of things to help you put on a top class show. Most things you can get for very little money – or even for free! – if you are prepared to hunt in garages, attics and at jumble sales. So start collecting things now! For **costumes** you'll need pieces of fabric, felt, wool and scarves. Modelling clay, empty fizzy drinks bottles and old gloves will all come in handy for making **props**. Big cardboard boxes and sheets are good for making **scenery** and backcloths. And you'll need paints and pens for decorating posters and masks. Look at the picture for more ideas.

DRAMA TIPS

Look out for helpful tips in the coloured strips down the side of each page.

You can find out more about the words that appear in **bold type** in the glossary at the back of the book.

old curtains or sheets

tape

pen poster

buttons

coconut

make-up

old sock

wig

mirror

cardboard chairs

cardboard box

bubble wrap

glove

paper plates

P.V.A glue

light

brush

torch

plastic bucket

wall-paper paste

string

scissors

coloured plastic

onion

sponge

newspapers

paints

balloon

5

Get your team together

Putting on a production needs teamwork. There are all sorts of jobs to do, so organize your crew right away.

I design the costumes

I build the sets

I'm the director

I'm an actor!

-To be or not to be...

I help out backstage

The director tells the actors which moves to make. The house manager collects tickets, and sells programmes and ice creams to the **audience**. The stage manager and stagehands look after the props and the sound crew look after sound effects and music. The costume designer decides what people will wear and the **set** designer is in charge of the scenery.

I collect tickets and sell ice cream

I'm in charge of sound effects

I'm the stage manager

I work the spotlight

More lipstick, please!

I put on the actors' make-up

The lighting designer makes sure the lighting is right. The make-up artist gives the actors fantastic-looking faces.

In a small **amateur** production, you might have to do more than one job. This is good because you'll learn more and discover which jobs you do and don't like.

Keeping a notebook

PROJECT

A drama notebook is very useful, whatever your role in a production. As you read through this book and do the projects, you will see that there are lots of things to remember – so let your notebook help! Write your **scripts** and **cast** lists in it and use it to plan your **rehearsal** schedule. Sketch out your ideas for costumes, scenery and make-up designs. Stick pictures of actors, TV stars and directors into it and write about why you like them.

A history of drama

Drama has been around for thousands of years! In every part of the world, audiences have always enjoyed watching people perform in all sorts of productions.

Here are some of my favourites!

8

Prehistoric people used drama as a kind of magic to help them catch animals.

American Western movies are full of exciting battles.

In medieval 'mystery' plays, good knights fought with evil dragons.

The ancient Greeks invented drama as we know it today, with a stage and actors.

William Shakespeare was a brilliant playwright who lived over 400 years ago – his plays are still performed all over the world.

Indonesian shadow puppets are controlled by sticks.

The actors in a Japanese Kabuki play wear fantastic costumes and make-up.

Henrik Ibsen's plays were the first to deal with the lives of ordinary people.

In the 1500s, people enjoyed watching the clowns of the Italian commedia dell'arte.

The dragons have become aliens and the 'knights' wear spacesuits in modern science fiction films.

Aphra Behn was the first woman to earn a living as a playwright.

Today, people enjoy watching the drama of TV soap operas.

9

If you see a mime artist giving a street performance, stop and have a look. Think about what it is that makes them so believable and pick up a few tips.

When you are miming eating, pretend you have got the food in your hand and really try to imagine what it is like to be eating it.

Warm up

A good actor must convince the audience that they are the person – or thing – they are pretending to be. And good acting starts with actions! Try some of these games to help you practise the art of **mime**. They are a great way of warming up *and* having some fun.

Mirroring

10

PROJECT

All actors have to work closely with other actors and be aware of what everyone else is doing on **stage**. This game is a fun way of practising the skills you need to work with other actors. Stand face to face with a partner. Slowly, one person starts to move their body into different positions. The other person must mirror their actions exactly. You might end up in some funny poses! Take it in turns to be the leader.

Imaginary Picnic

PROJECT

This is a game for two or more people. Take about twenty small pieces of paper and write the name of a different food on each. For example, a banana, an ice cream or some spaghetti. Fold up the pieces of paper and put them in a box. The first person picks out a piece of paper and then mimes eating the food written on it. The person who guesses the food mimes next.

Crazy machine

PROJECT

You'll need several people for this noisy, fun project. Standing in a line, the first person chooses a machine noise with a movement to go with it. The next person follows with a different noise and movement. As each person chooses a new sound and action, the effect of a huge jerky machine is created. Try going round in a circle, getting faster and faster until the machine explodes!

AAAAA

E-E-E-R-K

BOOM

S-S-S-T!

Try the art of hand dancing! Flap and flutter your hands like a bird or a butterfly. Then clap or tap them to the rhythm of a strong beat. Try being the hands of a pianist, a typist and then a person sewing.

Jot down in your drama notebook which music best suits each type of movement.

Try making a video of your acting projects – it's fun to watch them afterwards.

Music and movement

Adding music to your acting will help you get carried away with your movements. You'll need a tape or CD player and some music that is suitable for each of these acting projects. Relax and try not to be self-conscious.

Dinosaur

PROJECT

Imagine you are a ferocious dinosaur – huge, heavy and very hungry! Stand tall and stomp around to some noisy pop music with pounding beats.

Pebble

PROJECT

Now you are a pebble on a beach. Start off rough and jagged, then as you are rolled by stormy seas, slowly become smooth and round. Choose swirling, splashy music for this.

Don't be shy! Enjoy yourself!

weather game

PROJECT

This is one to test your imagination. Wind, rain, snow and sunshine all have different moods. Choose a piece of music and then transform yourself into a type of weather to suit it. Can your friends guess which weather you are?

Cobra

13

PROJECT

Become a hissing, creeping cobra – poisonous and dangerous and slithering around people's ankles and feet! What sort of music would be good for this?

Practise your expressions and emotions in a mirror. To help yourself act happy, think about getting a lovely present. To act sad, think about your goldfish dying!

If your character has to cry in a play but you can't get the tears to flow, try chopping up an onion and sniffing it before you go on stage — it's sure to get the waterworks going!

You can use grown-up shoes to help you act a character but make sure you pad them out with cotton wool and be very careful walking.

Learning to act

The key to putting on a good play is to have believable **characters** and an interesting story. Try some of these projects to get you started.

Young and old

Practise acting different characters. Studying the **gestures** and **expressions** of real people will help you in your acting. You may need to exaggerate their characteristics for effect.

PROJECT

Try acting the character of a baby. She will have a high voice and fall over easily. An old person might be bent over and have a shaky voice and movements.

Talking stone

PROJECT

You need a stone that's nice to hold and a few friends. Sit in a ring. The person holding the pebble starts to make up a story, then after a few sentences passes the stone to the next person. They pick up the story for a few more sentences before passing it on again. Listen carefully, it could be your turn at any time!

Happy or sad

PROJECT

Practise acting emotions by choosing a simple sentence like, 'What's in the box?' and saying it as if your character is happy. Now say it angrily, sadly and nervously.

Tricks of the trade!

Sometimes actors have to act things that they wouldn't want to do for real – like hitting someone! So, every actor has a few tricks up their sleeve to fool the audience.

Safe punching

The art of theatrical fighting is called **stage combat**. Although two actors can appear to be fighting, they are probably performing an illusion which tricks the audience into believing their punches are for real.

You must never hit someone – the whole point of acting is to pretend!

1. fist stops here ↓

2. POW!

3.

PROJECT

The main rule of stage combat is 'safety first'. So be careful not to hurt yourself or other people.

1. The 'attacker' stands just over an arm's length away from the 'receiver'.

2. When making the blow, the attacker's fist misses the receiver's face by several centimetres. At exactly the same time, the attacker slaps her shoulder or chest, which makes a thump.

3. The receiver acts as if he has just been hit – and the audience is completely fooled!

Breaking a fall!

1.

PROJECT

If you are involved in stage combat, you might have to fall over. This will make the fight look more realistic and is exciting for the audience. However, it is important to learn to 'break' your fall, or to fall without hurting yourself. Practise in an open space, such as a lawn, away from any hard objects.

1. If you are falling to the right, first move your right foot behind your left foot by about 20cm. When you start to fall, put most of your weight on the outside of your right foot.

2.

2. As you fall, curl the outside of the ankle, calf, knee and thigh of your right leg towards the ground. This will help to absorb the impact as your body drops downwards.

3.

DRAMA TIPS

Try kissing someone who is not there – James Bond used this trick to escape from a pursuer! With your back to the audience, cross your arms in front of your chest then run your hands up and down your back.

17

Burping, sneezing, snoring, hiccuping, coughing and yawning are all things that we do naturally, without thinking about them. Doing them on stage, on **cue**, *is surprisingly difficult. If they don't mind, practise these actions in front of a friend. Try to find ways of making them seem realistic.*

3. Land on your right arm and forearm, tucking your head onto the shoulder and bicep. If you are pretending to be dead, remember to keep very still! Practise your falls on both sides many times before you perform them on stage.

DRAMA TIPS

Charlie Chaplin starred in silent movies in the 1920s. His badly-fitting clothes and waddling walk made him one of the world's all-time favourite comedians.

*Telling jokes is guaranteed to make people laugh but stick to short jokes as they are easier to remember. Use puppets to tell your jokes (see pages 20-21 for how to make puppets) and set up a mini **comedy** show in your sitting room.*

Here are some jokes to get you started:
Q: What do you give a sick pig?
A: Oink-ment

Q: What do you call a man with a seagull on his head?
A: Cliff

Who is your favourite comedian? What is it about them that makes you laugh? It might be the things they say or do, and it might also be the clothes they wear. Have a go at these projects to make an audience laugh.

Silly walks

PROJECT

Moving your body in a funny way will give people a giggle.

There are a host of silly walks to try. Waddle like a duck, hop like a kangaroo, stride like a soldier or tiptoe like a dancer. Think up your own silly walks too.

Custard pie

PROJECT

The actors in a pantomime or a circus often perform **slapstick** comedy. They hit their heads, fall over, get soaked with water – and the audience loves it! A paper plate and a dollop of canned UHT cream make a great comedy custard pie. But remember, only push it in the face of somebody that is expecting it. Their job is to act shocked – you shouldn't surprise them for real!

squirty cream

paper plates

Funny glasses

pingpong balls

1.

2.

glue

toy glasses

pens

PROJECT

These whacky specs are definitely good for a laugh.

1. Using thick marker pens, draw red 'veins' and a black dot 'pupil' on two ping-pong balls.

2. Stick them to the front of a pair of toy glasses. (Don't walk in these specs, you might trip over – which wouldn't be very funny for you!)

Funny clothes can help your comedy

Your favourite sports or pop star can appear in your puppet theatre. Stick their photo onto card then cut round the edge. Tape a straw or a stick to the back.

Puppets

A puppet show is one of the oldest forms of theatre. People were putting on puppet shows in Ancient Egypt, Ancient Greece and India more than 2,000 years ago.

Sock puppets

PROJECT

You can create all sorts of puppets from just a few old socks. Take the first sock and, to give your puppet eyes, sew two buttons onto the heel. For a nose, glue or sew scraps of felt to the toe, then stick on a tongue and ears. Use felt and buttons of different colours and shapes to make a whole zoo of creatures.

fabric glue

buttons

felt

needle

old sock

20

Finger puppets

PROJECT

This is a way of making a complete cast of characters – on just one hand! Take an old glove – woollen or rubber – and with just a few bits of felt, card, string and wool, make each finger into a little person. Draw on faces and give them different clothes and hairstyles.

string

card

fabric glue

felt

wool

pen

Make a puppet theatre

PROJECT

Build this theatre so your puppets have a stage for their show.

1. Draw out the shape of the theatre on the bottom of a cardboard box. With an adult's help, cut along your lines.

2. Tape some strips of fabric to the inside of the box. These are your curtains. They don't need to close, they just help the box look like a real theatre.

3. Paint the inside of the box black and decorate the outside with brightly coloured paints, adding the finer details with a marker pen.

4. Stand your theatre on a table or on another box with plenty of room behind. Now you are ready to give a puppet show! Get your puppets to act out a fairy story, or to sing in silly voices.

cardboard box

scissors tape

paints

pen

brush

fabric

21

Making a play

Creating your own play can be very exciting. You'll need to come up with an entertaining story and some strong characters. Try to keep it short and to think of a good ending.

Mini plays

PROJECT

Before you write anything, try some **improvisation** with a friend. Pick different characters and then, using just a few props, make up the words and actions as you go along. You never know what might happen!

22

Write a script

PROJECT

From your improvised mini plays you can work out a good idea for a proper play. You will need to write or type the play in the form of a script. A script tells the cast and crew where the play is set and what characters are in it. It must also tell the actors what they have to say and do. Keep the story simple and avoid any long speeches by your characters. Here is an idea for a play in case you get stuck.

THE STRANGE PET

Scene: A veterinary surgery

Cast: Ms Macdonald, the vet (wearing a white coat)
Mr Brown, a customer (wearing overalls)
Matilda, his pet monster (scary-looking, with big teeth)

Vet (cheerily): "Good morning, Mr Brown."

Mr Brown (grumpily): "It's Matilda, she's got toothache and
I want you to fix it!"

Matilda: "OOOWWWWWW!!"

Vet (terrified): "Oh, err...excuse me a minute!"
(She dashes out screaming.)

THE END

DRAMA TIPS

Invent other funny
characters and their weird
pets to visit the vet.

Think up some more plays.
Here are some ideas
to get you started:

● The witches' repair shop
– a witch walks in with her
broken broom...

● The football trials – one
of the players is a girl...

● On board an
old-fashioned sailing ship –
the captain spots a pirate
ship in the distance...

The dress rehearsal is the last rehearsal before the first performance. It gives the actors the chance to wear their costumes on stage for the first time – and to check that they work with the sets!

Actors are very superstitious – they believe it is bad luck to wish another actor good luck. Instead they say 'break a leg' to each other before they go on stage.

24

Rehearsals

Once you have got a script, it's time to begin rehearsing the play. Rehearsals are important for everyone. The actors must work out their characters and the director has to decide what moves they will make. The **backstage** crew should practise working with the props, scenery and lights so that everything runs smoothly.

Speak on cue

Each actor must speak on cue, in other words, to talk at the moment they are supposed to! Your cue to speak may be the last words someone else has spoken, or they may be a sound effect made off stage.

Learn your lines

PROJECT

At first, the actors will read from their scripts in rehearsals. However, it is important that every actor eventually learns the words, known as **lines**, for their part. Remembering your lines can be tricky so get a friend to test you by reading out your cues.

Auditions

PROJECT

Sometimes the director holds an audition to choose the best person for each part. If you have to do an audition, learn a poem or a short speech from a play to perform.

Break a leg!

Face the front!

PROJECT

When you are speaking on stage, try to face the audience – it looks better and helps your voice **project** across the theatre. (Imagine that you are talking to a deaf old lady sitting in the back row!) Finally, don't forget to think about what the words mean, and to say them with the right kind of feeling.

*Many professional theatres have curtains that hang at the sides of the stage in the **wings**. They prevent the audience from seeing behind stage from their seats in the auditorium.*

Also backstage are the dressing rooms, workshops and wardrobe rooms used by the cast and crew.

26

Create a dappled light effect on a wall with a bowl of water, a mirror and a torch. Angle the mirror under the water then shine the torch at the mirror and tap the edge of the bowl.

Backstage

Without backstage helpers, a performance cannot go ahead. Taking part backstage is great fun and there are plenty of jobs to choose from. Just like the actors, the backstage crew must practise their actions, and listen for the cues that signal them to start.

Lighting

PROJECT

The atmosphere of a stage set relies very much on the lighting. The lighting designer must think about what mood they need to create and what effects they want to use. Many scenes just need a bright, natural light, but to create different moods, place coloured transparent plastic sheets in front of a light. For a spooky effect, hold a torch under your chin.

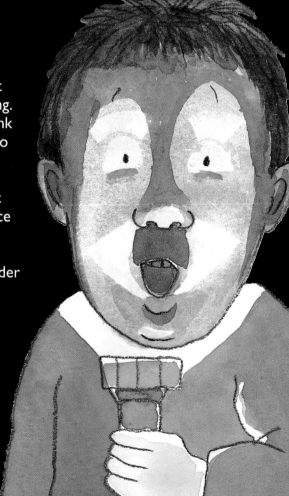

Close the curtains

Curtains keep the audience from seeing the scenery being changed. Practise opening and closing them with style!

Moving props

PROJECT

For a show to run smoothly you need a team of stagehands to move the props and scenery on and off stage between scenes. The props should be kept on tables at either side of the stage so they can be found easily when they are needed. When moving scenery, it is important to be as quick and as quiet as possible. Stagehands usually wear black clothes so they cannot be seen by the audience.

Prompting

PROJECT

Sometimes when people are nervous on stage, they forget their lines. This is known as **drying up**. Because of this, someone should be in the wings following the script all the way through the play. If an actor dries up, the **prompter** can whisper the next line to them.

DRAMA TIPS

Dolls make good baby props. You can record the voice of a real baby and use it as a sound effect if you need to. (See pages 38-39 for making sound effects.)

Scenery and props

Are you planning to put on a mystery or a comedy? Perhaps you'll do a famous play like *Toad of Toad Hall*. Whatever your show, you will need scenery to create atmosphere and props to help the action.

Make a mobile phone

PROJECT

A telephone is a useful prop, and what better than an up-to-date mobile phone? Wrap an empty chocolate box in black paper and attach a straw to the top with modelling clay. Cut out some small squares of yellow paper and arrange them as buttons on the front.

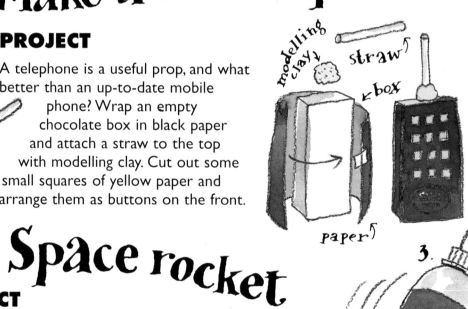

modelling clay

straw

box

paper

Space rocket

PROJECT

1. Make this space rocket from one large plastic drinks bottle and two small ones. Wrap each bottle in coloured paper.
2. Paint on windows and glue the 'boosters' to the 'rocket'.
3. Attach a piece of string to the top and you have lift-off!

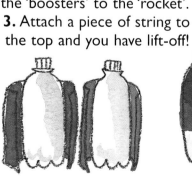

1.
2.
3.

28

Magic forest

PROJECT

Cut up some large cardboard boxes into grass and tree shapes. For your scenery to stand up, create 'feet' out of rectangles of card. Cut slits in the base of the scenery and in the feet, as shown in the diagram above. Finally, paint your scenery in greens, browns and purples for a really magical effect.

Backcloth

PROJECT

The backcloth hangs at the rear of the stage and is used to set the scene. An old piece of fabric, some camouflage netting or a shower curtain will do very well. For a night scene, use a dark blue backcloth with small holes dotted all over it. Shine a light behind it and you have starlight!

Making a meal out of it!

PROJECT

Sometimes it is not possible to use real objects on stage and so props must be faked. Food, for example, would get very smelly if you used it night after night. So make life-like meals from modelling clay, dried food and other materials, and glue them to paper plates.

glue

modelling clay

paper plates

rice

cotton wool

dried peas

DRAMA TIPS

Corrugated cardboard sprayed with silver metallic paint is good for making swords and shields.

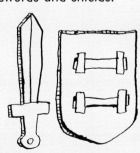

Costume

Dressing up in a costume helps the audience recognise the character that you are playing. Hunt around your house and at car boot sales for all the old clothes you can find, then start up a costume collection in a big box. Look out for scarves, hats and pieces of fabric.

old coat

King or Queen

PROJECT

For that 'royal' look, a big fake fur coat is a good place to start. Next, cut out a crown from some yellow card. To finish off, add some chunky jewellery.

yellow card

scissors

glove

string

toilet paper

orange card

tape

Be a cockerel

PROJECT

Transform yourself into a red rooster! Take an old rubber glove, attach two strings to either side of the cuff and then stuff it with toilet paper. Next, take a triangle of orange card and tape it into a cone shape. Attach some elastic or string to each side.

Cock-a-doodle-doo!

Make a horse

PROJECT

1. Flatten out a cardboard box into a rectangle and cut out the shape shown on the diagram. Cut along the solid lines shown, and fold along the dotted ones. Draw on the horse's features.

2. Tape the head and neck together at an angle and tape on a pair of cardboard ears.

3. Two people, a big sheet and a tail … and your horse is finished!

42 cm   42 cm

20 cm   20 cm   20 cm   60 cm

scissors

pen

1.

2.

3.

wool or string

tape

coconut

toy bird sewed on

Easy tunic

55 cm

PROJECT

Take a piece of fabric 55cm wide and 150cm long. Cut a 20cm hole in the middle. Put your head through the hole and fasten a belt around your waist.

150 cm

This tunic can be adapted to make all sorts of costumes. Try sewing beads or scraps of material to it. You can even attach a parrot to it if you are playing the part of a pirate!

DRAMA TIPS

A scarf can be folded in different ways to make all sorts of costumes.

31

Have fun with your masks and decorate them with glitter, feathers, glow-in-the-dark paint, shiny stars and even leaves.

Masks

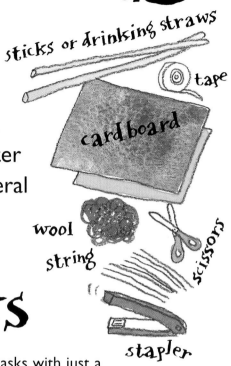

One minute you can be a clown, the next you can be an animal – wearing a mask is a great way of 'becoming' a character and means you can act several parts in a play.

sticks or drinking straws

tape

cardboard

wool

string

scissors

stapler

Stick masks

PROJECT

Make animal, monster or human face masks with just a few bits and bobs. Cut out different mask shapes in cardboard and give them eye-holes. Staple on ears, hair and other features. For a handle, tape a stick to the back.

Papier mâché mask

PROJECT

1. Mix up the wallpaper paste with water so it has the consistency of thick cream. Blow up the balloon and rip the newspaper into strips. One by one, dip each strip into the paste mix and stick onto the balloon. After one layer, hang the balloon up and leave to dry. Repeat this process until you have about eight layers.

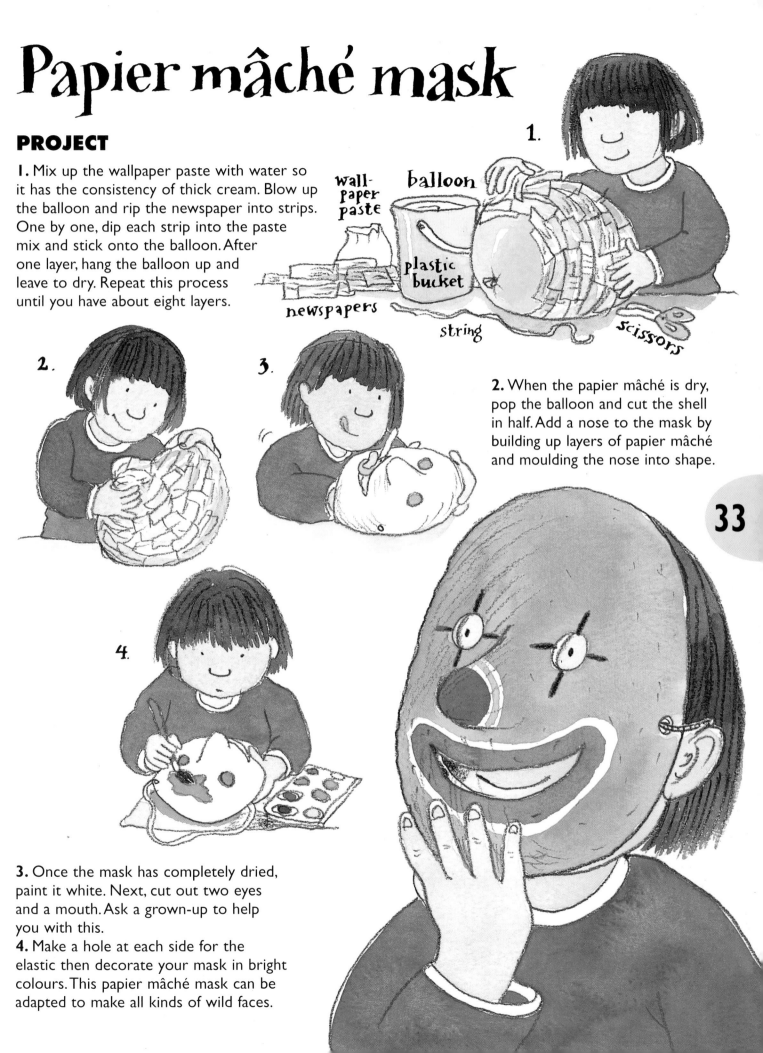

2. When the papier mâché is dry, pop the balloon and cut the shell in half. Add a nose to the mask by building up layers of papier mâché and moulding the nose into shape.

33

3. Once the mask has completely dried, paint it white. Next, cut out two eyes and a mouth. Ask a grown-up to help you with this.

4. Make a hole at each side for the elastic then decorate your mask in bright colours. This papier mâché mask can be adapted to make all kinds of wild faces.

DRAMA TIPS

Give yourself knobbly monster-legs by wearing a pair of coloured tights and stuffing them with screwed-up blobs of toilet paper or newspaper.

To create false ears, attach cardboard shapes to an Alice band.

False parts

Transform yourself into all sorts of weird and wonderful characters with these false parts. A few bits and bobs and a little imagination – and even your friends won't recognise you!

Scary hands

PROJECT

1. Put a pair of washing-up gloves or gardening gloves on some newspaper. Fluff up some black wool and glue it to the back of the gloves.

2. Cut ten, egg-shaped claws from card and paint them with nail varnish.

3. When the nail varnish is dry, stick the cardboard claws onto the gloves. AARRGH!

nail varnish · card · gloves · wool · scissors · P.V.A glue

1. · 2. · 3.

Ugly nose

PROJECT

This horrible hooter is sure to give your audience a fright!

1. Cover the inner tube of a toilet roll with papier mâché using the technique described on page 33. Give the nose a lumpy texture by adding gluey blobs of paper to each layer.

2. Block up just one end of the tube and when it is half dry, make the nostrils by poking a pencil through the blocked end.

3. Once dry, paint the nose and add modelling clay warts. Finally, fasten on some elastic to the open end.

1.

2.

3.

Woolly beard

PROJECT

1. Cut out a semi-circle of thin cardboard and, with adult help, cut out a mouth in the middle. Make two holes at either corner.

2. Glue on some wool around the 'chin'.

3. Thread some elastic through the holes and knot the ends. Draw on some red lips with a marker pen.

1.

2.

3.

Baldy head

PROJECT

1. For this project, use either a pink swimming cap or a bald cap from a novelty store. Ask an adult to make a row of small holes around the bottom edge of the cap with a needle. Carefully thread some wool through each of the holes.

2. Tie a knot at the end of each piece of wool inside the cap.

3. Put the cap on your head and be prepared for a shock!

1.

2.

3.

35

Make-up

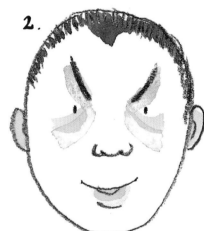

water-based face paints

brushes

sponges

water

When you have chosen your costume, think about what make-up should go with it. Is your character scary, weird, glamorous or funny? You will need a selection of water-based face paints, some sponges, brushes and water.

Evil vampire

PROJECT

1. Apply a light brown base coat with a dry sponge. Next, paint on white highlights along the eyebrows, cheekbones, nose and chin then blend in with a sponge.

1.

2.

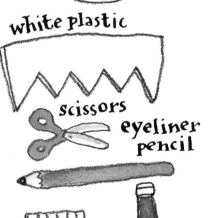

white plastic

36

2. Use black paint to make angled eyebrows and a widow's peak. Then give yourself shadows around the eyes. Grease back your hair with hair gel.

3. Make a row of fangs by cutting them out from a washing-up liquid bottle. Add a few scars with an eyeliner pencil and some fake tomato ketchup blood to finish.

scissors

eyeliner pencil

hair gel

tomato ketchup

3.

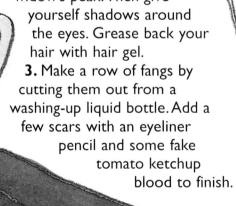

Space invader

PROJECT

How about being a three-eyed, two-mouthed monster from outer space?

1. Pull your hair back into a tight ponytail. Apply white paint patches around the eyes.

1.

2. Paint two lines around the eyes, two red patches for mouths, and make the rest of the face green. For the head, either stuff a shower cap with toilet paper or else use a green swimming cap.

2.

3. Cut out an oval-shaped piece of card and give it a black rim and a pupil, to match your real eyes. A bubble wrap cloak will finish off the costume and really make you look 'out of this world'!

3.

bubble wrap ↘

DRAMA TIPS

Sometimes it is easier to get someone else to do your make-up.

The effects you make should be bold and dramatic, so even the people in the back row can see them.

If you have made any of the false parts from pages 34-35, blend them into your face with make-up of the same colour.

Gently wash off your make-up with soap and water.

37

Sound

Sound is a very important part of drama. As well as the voices of the actors, a play might need sound effects and music. Some drama, such as a radio play, can be created using only sound.

Make a radio play

PROJECT

To record a radio play, you will need a tape recorder with a built-in microphone, a quiet room and a lot of imagination. Plan your script using the techniques described on pages 22-23, but remember that the audience cannot see the action. So everything that happens must be described by the actors or made using a sound effect. Use music to create atmosphere.

Sound effects

There are two kinds of sound effect – the sort you do live backstage, as the play is happening, and the sort that you record beforehand and then play back when you need it.

1. crunch

2. thunder

Live

PROJECT

1. A baking tray of gravel can be used for someone walking up a garden path.
2. A sheet of cardboard or hardboard makes thunder.
3. Pop a paper bag for gunshot.
4. Two halves of a coconut are great for horses' hooves.
5. A bucket of water is useful for any water sound effects.

3. BANG!

4.

5. splish splash

clip clop

1. bizz! bizz!

Recorded

PROJECT

Some sounds are difficult to fake so must be recorded.
1. A doorbell
2. Birdsong
3. A creaky door
4. A barking dog
5. The chimes of a grandfather clock

2. tweet tweet tweet

ding dong

5.

3. creak

4.

woof!

39

In the movie world, filming is known as 'shooting' and shooting each scene is called 'doing a take'.

Most films or TV shows are not filmed in the order you see them. The shots are pieced, or 'cut', together later.

Making movies

Y ou have probably watched drama on a screen – either on television or as a film at the cinema. Soon you'll have a chance to make a movie of your own, but first it's a good idea to find out a bit more about how screen drama is made.

When you watch a film or a TV show, notice how the same object can be shot from different angles for different effects.

In a similar way, the director will choose to use a close-up or a 'long shot' (a shot from a long distance) to look at an object.

Watch TV

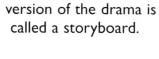

PROJECT

Watch an episode from a TV soap opera. Then, on one piece of paper, draw pictures to describe the story that you have seen. Try to show only the important moments – the bones of the story. This comic strip version of the drama is called a storyboard.

1. Spaceship lands
2. Alien!
3. Chicken
4. Face to face
5. Alien terrified of chicken!
6. Alien escapes

41

Storyboard your own movie!

PROJECT

Many movies start on a storyboard. These picture plans are a great help to the director and the actors. To storyboard your own movie, start by drawing small boxes on paper, then work out the main action of your film. Let's take the idea of an alien landing:

1. An alien rocket touches down on Earth.
2. The extra-terrestrial takes his first steps outside his ship.
3. Close by, a chicken is searching for food.
4. A close encounter of the feathery kind!
5. The chicken thinks the alien looks very tasty.
6. The alien escapes in his spaceship.

Now you can begin to make your movie!

Always make sure you ask before you borrow a video camera, and take great care of it. Ask the owner to show you how it works and get them to switch it to autofocus.

Silent movie

Lights …Camera …Action! Yes, it's time to shoot your own movie. This is going to be a silent movie, so you can call out directions as you shoot. For the final film show, you should turn down the sound and play music to go with the action.

If you can borrow a video camera it's time to have a go!

Make a silent film

PROJECT

For this project you will need to borrow a video camera. Start by planning your film with a storyboard (see pages 40-41).

42

Next, set up the props and scenery and rehearse the scene with the actors. They should practise their moves and expressions and the cameraperson must work out the shots he or she is going to take. Once you have filmed each shot, stop the tape and move on to the next one.

wrong

wrong

right

When filming, make sure you have the object you want to film in the middle of the viewfinder. Try to hold the camera still and not to tip it from side to side.

Each shot should be just a few seconds long. This keeps your film short and snappy, which is more interesting for the audience.

Use the zoom as little as possible and don't wave the camera around whilst you are filming (this is called 'hosepiping') – it looks really boring!

43

Signs and bubbles

PROJECT

Signs showing the name of the film, 'Scene 1' or 'The End' are fun to add to your shots. Speech bubbles cut out from card and taped to sticks can also add humour. **Professional** film-makers use a clapperboard at the beginning and end of each shot. Make one of your own from cardboard and a paper fastener.

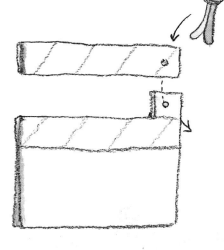

Old sheets or shower curtains hung from a clothesline make good front curtains.

Preparing for a Show

Choose which part of the book you've enjoyed the most and then put on a show for your friends and family. Whatever you pick, there are a few things to get ready before the the big performance.

Outdoor theatre

PROJECT

First, you need to find a place to put on your show. You could pick somewhere outside, with nature as your backcloth. Choose a safe area on the beach, in the countryside or in your garden. You might want to base your play around the animals found there.

Programme

PROJECT

Design programmes to hand out to each member of the audience.

1. Put the name of the show on the front cover. Inside, list the scenes, the cast of characters and the names of the actors. You should also credit everybody else who worked on the show.
2. Make double-sided photocopies of the programmes.
3. Fold each programme in half.

Poster

PROJECT

Put up posters to let everyone know about the performance. Make sure you put the name of the show, where and when it is to take place and the price of the tickets.

Tickets

PROJECT

Cut out tickets from card for the house manager to sell on the door. Give the tickets numbers and make sure that you have enough seats for every ticket. You could give the money you raise to charity.

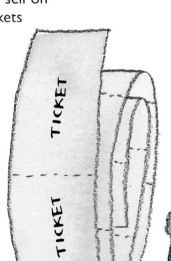

DRAMA TIPS

Have an interval halfway through the show. Serve juice and biscuits.

Interval 10 mins

Ask someone to take photos of the show, then you can stick them in your drama notebook.

The show

This is your chance to show everyone what you can do. Have fun! Oh yes…and break a leg!

Glossary

Amateur
Someone who takes part in a play for fun and does not get paid.

Audience
The people who watch a show.

Backstage
The area behind the stage, where the audience cannot see.

Cast
The actors in a play.

Character
A person in a play, the part played by an actor.

Comedy
A funny play with a happy ending, the opposite of a tragedy.

Costume
The clothes worn by actors on stage.

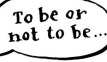

To be or not to be...

Cue
The signal for an actor to speak.

Drying up
Forgetting your lines on stage.

Expression
A look on an actor's face to show feelings.

Gesture
The movements of the hands, arms and body to show feelings.

Improvisation
Performing without preparation, making the words up as you go along.

Lines
The words that an actor speaks in a play.

Mime
Acting without words.

Professional
Someone who is paid for taking part in a show – it is their job.

Project
To talk clearly and loudly so everyone in the audience can hear.

Prompter
The person who whispers an actor's words to them if they forget them.

Props
Short for properties, props are the objects on stage used by the actors during the play.

Rehearsal
A practice session.

Set
The place that represents where a scene happens.

Scenery
The stage decorations that show where the play is set.

Script
The written words of a play.

Slapstick
Comedy using lots of clowning and silly antics.

Stage
The platform that the set stands on.

Stage combat
Carefully rehearsed fighting that looks realistic but does not hurt the actors.

Tragedy
A serious play with a sad ending.

Wings
The sides of the stage.

47

Drama School

Certificate

You have completed

Drama School

with excellence

Brita Granström – Tutor

Brita Granström